FUNNY FUNERALS

FUNNY FUNERALS

Byron Holtsclaw

To order additional copies of this book, contact:
Xlibris
1-888-795-4274
www.Xlibris.com
Orders@Xlibris.com
727937

TABLE OF CONTENTS

Dedication

In honor of my late father, Charles Edward Holtsclaw, who had a great sense of humor. He showed me the value of not taking oneself too seriously. Knowing him all my life I trust that he would have found a few unplanned events during his own funeral quite humorous. During his 12 mile funeral procession to the cemetery, the hearse lost power 20 times causing the procession to get down to a speed of 10 miles per hour on the highway for much of the journey. One particular lady must have been tired of waiting as she passed nearly a mile of the cars in the procession at a high rate of speed, including the hearse and firetruck leading the long procession. After the graveside service the hearse had to be towed back to town. It was later determined that one of the battery terminals had completely broken off on a second battery in the back of the hearse. Every time the hearse hit a bump in the road the electrical connection was lost and the engine would die. Until my father's service the funeral director was unaware the second battery existed.

Charles Edward Holtsclaw

Special Thanks

To the staff at Lester Jenkins & Sons Funeral Home in Bloomfield, IN who have always been so gracious to my family in our times of loss.

Serving Since 1925

Very Special Thanks

To James and Margaret Pirkle who ministered to the people of Washington, IN for 40 years as they owned and operated Gill Service, the oldest continuing business in Daviess County. Jim's professionalism and generosity set him apart in funeral service. Jim also served the congregation of First Christian Church as a deacon and chairman of the board. I had the privilege of ordaining him as an elder in 2008.

Jim & Margaret Pirkle

Introduction

All of us have come to grips with the reality by now that not one of us will escape this world without experiencing the certainty of death and paying taxes. As a minister of the Gospel of Christ I am humbled by the realities of this world. In Paul's letter to the Romans, he states the cause of the reality in this world, *"For the wages of sin is death, but the gift of God is eternal life in Christ Jesus our Lord."* I pray that I have been a vessel of God's mercy and compassion for the hundreds of families I have ministered to during their time of loss. For those who are still living on this earth, I pray that all would:

HEAR THE GOSPEL

> *(Romans 10:14, Acts 2:38, Acts 8:12, Acts 8:35, Acts 9:18, Acts 10:48, Acts 16:14, Acts 16:29, Acts 18:8, Acts 19:4, and Acts 22:7)*

BELIEVE THAT JESUS IS THE CHRIST

(Romans 10:9, Acts 2:38, Acts 8:12, Acts 8:35, Acts 9:18, Acts 10:48, Acts 16:14, Acts 16:29, Acts 18:8, Acts 19:4 and Acts 22:7)

CONFESS PUBLICALLY THAT JESUS IS THE CHRIST

(Romans 10:9, Acts 9:18, Acts 10:48, Acts 16:14, and Acts 22:7)

REPENT OF SIN

(Acts 2:38, Acts 2:38, Acts 9:18, Acts 16:29, Acts 19:4 and Acts 22:7 II Peter 3:9)

BE BAPTIZED

(Matthew 3:13, Matthew 28:18, John 3:5, Acts 2:38, Acts 8:12, Acts 8:35, Acts 9:18, Acts 10:48, Acts 16:14, Acts 16:29, Acts 18:8, Acts 19:4, Acts 22:7, Romans 6:3, I Corinthians 10:2, Galatians 3:27, I Peter 3:21)

Our daughter, Liberty's baptism

I have found myself entertaining family and friends with these stories around the dinner table for years. All of these tales are true. There is no need to embellish any of these events. You simply cannot make up stuff like this. We have all experienced Murphy's Law: If it can go wrong, it will go wrong! I have officiated funeral services in dozens of locations. In order to protect people's privacy, names have been changed. If you recognize someone's name it is because the individual has given me permission to use their name. These short stories are a sample of the many comical experiences I've had over the years. If anyone is interested, there is a lot more where this came from. Please join me in appreciating the lighter side of life.

Seth, Liberty and Charlie have a great sense of humor

Larger Than Life

Many people make funeral arrangements with their local director well before their time of passing. In fact, I recommend that everyone prearrange their funeral service. Most people are shocked at the cost of a funeral when they pay the bill. As I write this, the average funeral in America has reached a cost of $10,000.00. Most people do not realize that today one can pre arrange their funeral service, locking in the cost of the service at the current price, freezing the expense at the current rate, without paying a penny at the time of the appointment.

Dottie was the oldest member in the congregation that I served. She was a single lady with a spunky personality. I greatly enjoyed every visit we ever had. You never knew what adolescent comment might come out of her mouth as she was always flirting with men. There was never a dull moment with Dottie.

She had told me that she had prearranged her funeral. Dottie went into great detail about a special request she had made with the funeral staff. I can remember as she was telling me the intimate details of her wishes, my face had become as red as a fire engine. She assured me that she was dead serious and that the staff at the funeral home had promised to honor her request. She even went to her closet to show me the extra-large garment she intended to have placed on her body for the day of her funeral.

The next day, my face again changed colors as I began to describe the conversation I had with Dottie to her good friend, our church secretary. "Well, Byron, that doesn't surprise me, knowing Dottie!" exclaimed our secretary with laughter.

Years had gone by and I had forgotten all about the awkward conversation years earlier. Dottie had suffered a stroke and had a short stay at the hospital before her passing. Her niece and accountant were there with me when she passed. A few days later, I led a time of prayer at the funeral chapel with her family before visitation began. I was seated at the back of the chapel when I looked up toward the casket. My eyes bulged out of my head when I noticed Dottie's blouse transcending out above the casket. After composing myself, I had a conversation with the funeral staff. A full box of Kleenex tissues had been used for each cup...just as Dottie had requested.

Needless to say, as I delivered the service that day from the podium at the funeral home my eyes stayed focused on the audience. Can you guess the topic of discussion by our church ladies at the funeral dinner that afternoon? All it took to spark the conversation was the size of the fried chicken. Everyone was amazed at the 2 large surprises Dottie had for everyone at her service.

During the dinner, our church secretary exclaimed, "Well, Byron, that doesn't surprise me, knowing Dottie!"

She Would Give You the Coat Off of Her Back

I have served in nearly every capacity during a funeral service, except as a funeral director. On one occasion my wife's family gave me the honor of serving as a pall bearer for a dear deceased family member. It was a cold February afternoon with a long funeral procession two counties away. Everyone had worn top coats to the cemetery and the wind was quite bitter. The vault company had a large tent erected over the burial site with a propane heater attempting to give the family some relief from the cold.

As the family made their way inside the tent, the director kept projecting, "Please come toward the heater!"

A few moments later, again, "Please come toward the heater!" exclaimed the funeral director.

Everyone packed in tight around the heater and the minister began the graveside service. Seconds later, the service was interrupted as Jan had backed the tail of her topcoat into the open flame of the propane heater. Everyone standing behind Jan saw what had happened as the flames climbed up the coat. For a moment, Jan was unaware of what was happening until the family fire department began making efforts to extinguish the raging blaze. Jan, with her cat like reflexes quickly took off her coat as family members put out the flames in the snow.

Praise the Lord, Jan was alright! After a few minutes of uncontrollable laughter, the minister resumed the service. All that was left of Jan's top coat were sleeves and a collar connecting them. Her fabric ignited like flash paper.

People like Jan will do anything for you, even if it means setting herself on fire to keep you warm on a cold day.

Larry and Janice Hicks

Unaccommodating Funeral Director

So many times when laying a loved one to rest the weather is most undesirable. I have compassion for folks who have to deal with the elements during their time of loss. On one such occasion it was the wishes of the deceased to be buried at a rural cemetery located on a hill. It was a bitter winter day. The entire service was to be at the cemetery. A small crowd had gathered and was waiting to start the service upon the arrival of family members from out of the area. The family traveling had called to say that they were running late. Everyone waiting was making every effort to tolerate the frigid temperature.

When the family finally arrived one of the survivors was a lady dressed in heels, a fur coat and huge diamonds dangling from her ears, neck and fingers. The funeral staff and I greeted the family at the burial tent and told them they could take a moment with their deceased loved one, as the casket was open, before I started the service.

After spending a moment at the casket, the lady in the fur coat began talking to the funeral director. The director began smiling and assuring the lady that everything was in order.

The lady wearing the fur coat then turned to me and pleaded, "Can we warm her up? Her hands are freezing!"

I then smiled at her much like the funeral director had and said, "Ma'am, her hands are freezing because it is very cold today."

"I know it is cold that's why I want to warm her up!" She rebutted.

"Can't we put a blanket on her to keep her warm?" The lady demanded.

The funeral director jumped to my defense, "Ma'am, we can put a blanked on her if you want to but it is not going to keep her warm!"

"And just why not?" She sneered

"Well, ma'am, you see your loved one is dead," stated the director.

Moments later I delivered a very warm message in honor of the deceased.

Burial at Sea

Tim was a hard worker and a loyal friend, but Tim had just one flaw. From the time he would get home from work to the time he would lay down to rest he always had a cold one in his hand. Each can was never in his hand long enough to get warm before Tim had emptied the can and replaced it with another. Day after day, week after week, month after month, year after year Tim's habits took a terrible toll on his body. Tim did not live to be very old when his funeral came to pass.

Tim's widow stood near his casket the night of his visitation. Neighbors, friends, coworkers and family all shared comforting thoughts with Tim's widow all evening long. Soon, Tim's drinking buddy arrived to pay his respects. In honor of Tim, his old pal continued right where Tim had left off with his beverages.

When he had made his way to the front of the chapel where Tim's widow was, he made a loud proclamation, "If we had all the beer Tim and I had drank together, why, we could float that casket right on out of here!"

At that, Tim's friend dismissed himself to refreshments at another venue.

Pretty Woman

I have officiated funerals with hundreds of folks in attendance. This was not one of those occasions. The widow of a late physician had passed away. She had outlived her husband by 30 years and wished to be brought back to the area to be laid to rest by his side at the cemetery. The only folks at the funeral were the daughter and granddaughter. Imagine me standing at the podium in the funeral chapel with only 2 ladies seated and an open casket. I gave a eulogy, sang hymns, prayed prayers and preached a sermon for these 2 grieving ladies.

As I was making my concluding remarks, a man whom I knew, walked into the chapel and made his way to the open casket.

I never paused giving my remarks to the ladies as the gentleman bent over the casket, kissing the deceased on the lips and shouted, "My god, you were a pretty woman!"

While I'm still talking, the man turns to the 2 ladies on the front row and begins loudly introducing himself to them. At this point, I pause before my prayer. About 4 minutes later, the gentleman shuts his mouth long enough that I chose to give the benediction.

Meanwhile, the funeral staff discovers that the daughter and granddaughter of the deceased have a flat tire on their car. The funeral home makes arrangements to have the local tire shop repair the tire during the funeral. Without cost, the funeral home offered to drive the 2 ladies to the cemetery in their limousine. I always tarry behind with the casket as the family makes their way to their transportation outside the funeral chapel. As I led the casket between the hearse and limo I was amazed to see the gentleman seated in the limo between both ladies with his arms around them.

Those ladies were so fortunate to be comforted by the gentleman that day. At least that's what I overheard him telling them at the cemetery.

The funeral staff member who drove the limo to the cemetery began telling me what he heard going on in the backseat in route to the burial. The limo driver knows me well and according to him, the gentleman in the backseat had made all kinds of outrageous claims about me to the ladies during the ride. I was deeply honored to be the subject of conversation.

As I am listening to this account of blaspheme, I see the gentleman showing the 2 ladies where his burial plot is and he tells them, "See, someday I'll be laying here right beside your momma and grandma."

How comforting.

Gun Show

Martin was a single man who lost his battle with cancer and passed away at an early age. He was an outdoorsman with a very nice gun collection. When he passed, the county sheriff and I took these firearms to the security center for safe keeping until they could be auctioned by Martin's sister at a later date. The sheriff and I were both good friends of Martin and had been with him during the long battle with cancer. We agreed to each have a part during our friend's funeral and began talking about what we would say. The sheriff had a very interesting idea of how to handle his portion of the service.

When it was the sheriff's time to speak he came to the pulpit dressed in his finest black suit. After he had spoken a few moments he reached in his jacket, removed his .44 caliber automatic pistol and set it down on the pulpit. Without pausing he continued speaking only to reach in the other side of his jacket, removing a .38 caliber revolver and set it down on the opposite side of the pulpit. Without blinking, the sheriff continued the eulogy as he pulled the .22 pistol from the back of his belt, slapping it down on the pulpit. 3 more pistols appeared out of the sheriff's suit and piled up on the church furniture as the eulogy continued; 6 pistols in all.

As he took the Remington 870 Express Pump and the AR-15 from the choir loft and leaned them against the pulpit, the sheriff explained that he and Martin would often go out to eat and at some point in the conversation Martin would ask, "Are you packing?"

They would then wait till the server returned and would start laying their guns out on the table in order to shock their server.

What kind of reaction would they get?

Usually a reaction just like all the guests at Martin's funeral had.

Martin L. Mumaw III and I.

How many turkeys do you see?

Police Work

I have a quirk about objects in my pockets while I teach. While I would preach on Sunday my wallet, phone and keys would be in the desk drawer in the church office. One Sunday, a church member told my wife that she saw someone wearing safety green come into the church office during the sermon. Her view was through the half inch space between the auditorium double doors.

After the service I returned to the church office and found the secretary's desk drawers all pulled out. Then the same in my office; my wallet was gone.

The next day I filed a police report. Church thefts are very common. There is a security camera pointed at the office entrance. The tape showed a man I knew, wearing safety green, entering the office door at 11:05 am (the start of my morning message) and exiting the building at 11:13 am. The man on camera was a known panhandler who would ask me for money every few months. Every Christmas he would show up after the service asking for money and would explain that his girlfriend was having a baby. The police told me that he had outstanding warrants for his arrest in 3 counties and that they would question him about the theft.

A few days later, while riding in the hearse during a funeral procession, I was telling the driver of the hearse my story. As we proceeded through an intersection guess who I saw on the street corner? Cell phones are great. That afternoon the police department questioned the man as to his whereabouts and if he had taken anything from the church. His girlfriend had told police that he left the house at 11:00 am and returned at 11:20 am. When pressured to confess the crime, he denied any involvement.

The man had been convicted of stealing from several area churches and individuals, including his mother. I had helped him many times and would have helped him the day of the theft if he had only asked.

Several years later, I received a phone call from the janitor of an area church. He was replacing the toilet in the men's restroom when he discovered my driver's license lodged inside. He asked if I had missed it. I told him the story about the disappearance of my wallet. He then asked why the license would have been at that church. I asked him if the substance abuse classes had met at his church and if the panhandler had attended.

"Yes, I remember him coming here for class. He must have tried to flush your wallet while he was here!" exclaimed the voice on the phone.

I wonder if his girlfriend ever had her baby?

I chose to keep a good attitude about the situation. When I had to go to the BMV to replace my operator's license, I posed as my wife's favorite super hero for the photo, the Wolverine. Always a great conversation piece when I show my ID.

Fender Bender

Todd gave me the most memorable rides in the hearse. Every time he made a right turn in route to the cemetery, he would misjudge the distance to the curb. The back right wheel would come up over the curb and back down again. This made for an eventful last journey for the deceased. As the hearse would go up and down the curb, I could hear the casket bouncing around in the back. Now you know why the inside of the lid of the casket is padded.

The journeys with Todd were always filled with conversation. Todd liked to vent his frustrations during the ride to the cemetery. One occasion he was wound so tight that he missed the entrance to the cemetery. I received a vocabulary lesson as he turned around. The expressions on the faces of the drivers in all of the cars following us in the procession were priceless as we passed them by. Just goes to show you that one can attend church every Sunday, but when you are on your way to be buried you can be lost!

On yet another occasion, Todd had dented the hearse on the entrance of the garage. I was standing outside the hearse surveying the damage to the front fender and car door as the casket was placed in the hearse. Todd came around and asked me if I could get in. With both hands I pulled the smashed fender away from the door as Todd opened it. The door now pinched behind the fender would not close. I held onto the door as we proceeded down the highway to the cemetery. Upon arrival at the cemetery, I was unable to open the door I had been holding shut because the fender had it pinched closed now. Climbing over the console and steering wheel was my escape route. Now that the door was shut, I really didn't want to pry the fender out again to get back to town and I didn't want to climb back over the steering wheel and console. Nor did I wish to ride where the casket usually bounces around. Thus, on the way home, I repented of how I arrived at the cemetery and found another method of transportation.

Jim Pirkle had beautiful hearses to transport loved ones.

What's Missing?

Ruby and her husband came to the funeral home with very heavy hearts to make arrangements for their deceased newborn twins. Ruby explained to the funeral director that she had recently delivered her son and daughter at the hospital when the children's untimely deaths occurred. The bodies had been sent to the state capital for reconstruction as the twin had been born disfigured. Ruby and her husband had given the children names and wished to invite friends and relatives to a funeral service that week.

The funeral director comforted the mourning couple and provided all of the arrangements they requested. Many friends and relatives called at the chapel to comfort and console Ruby in light of this tragedy. 30 floral arrangements were sent from friends of the family. Thousands of dollars were donated to the family by area businesses and friends to help cover the family's expenses. A large attendance was present for the minister's remarks during the funeral. The community embraced Ruby and loved her in her time of need.

Weeks passed by and the funeral director began wondering why the bodies of the children had never been delivered to the funeral home to be buried. The funeral director called every hospital in the area. No one had ever heard of Ruby, nor had there been any infant deaths recently. Soon, the State Police investigated what had happened. The florist had no complaints.

Father Forgive Them

Dawn, a Catholic friend of mine was laid to rest very early in her adult life. I attended her funeral service at her parish. The priest gave a beautiful eulogy, we sang hymns, and we were comforted by special music and scripture. Only one thing was out of order. My friend's name wasn't Dawn. For over an hour, my late friend's family listened to their priest talk about someone named Dawn. My friend's name may have never dawned upon the priest, but somewhere a lady named Dawn has already been given her last rites.

What's His Name?

Reading the daily obituaries has become a part of my daily routine as on many occasions my name has been printed in an obituary that I was officiating, without anyone contacting me. My current record is 20 minutes notice before the service. To my knowledge, I have yet to miss a funeral that I was supposed to officiate.

I have also learned to be very liberal about claiming my name. You see, many folks have much difficulty with the spelling of my name.

The following is a partial list of how my name has appeared in printed obituaries.

Pastor Brian Holtslam

Brother Baron Holtsclaw

Rev. Bryan Holsopple

Bro. Bryon Holtsclaw

Pastor Byron Hostetter

Rev. Byron Holtzclaw

Rev. Bryan Holtclaw

Pastor Bryon Holstine

Rev. Byron Holt

Rev. Byron Holsclaw

Pastor Bryan Holtsclaws

Pastor Byron Holtsclaw

Which name is correct?

None of the above.

"What do you want to be called?" people ask.

Whatever you want to call me, just

don't call me late for dinner!

To my beautiful wife, Lora, whom I do not deserve:
you have prepared countless wonderful meals only to
eat them alone because I was ministering to others.

Our Hope

The Apostle Paul wrote to the Christians at Thessalonica:

"Brothers, we do not want you to be ignorant about those who fall asleep, or to grieve like the rest of men, who have no hope. We believe that Jesus died and rose again and so we believe that God will bring with Jesus those who have fallen asleep in him. According to the Lord's own word, we tell you that we who are still alive, who are left till the coming of the Lord, will certainly not precede those who have fallen asleep. For the Lord himself will come down from heaven, with a loud command, with the voice of the archangel and with the trumpet call of God, and the dead in Christ will rise first. After that, we who are still alive and are left will be caught up together with them in the clouds to meet the Lord in the air. And so we will be with the Lord forever. Therefore encourage each other with these words." – 1 Thessalonians 4:13-18

Edwards Brothers Malloy
Thorofare, NJ USA
September 14, 2016